◇AUTUMN◇ ACTIVITIES

Written by Denise Bieniek
Illustrated by Laura Ferraro

Troll Associates

Metric Conversion Chart

1 inch = 2.54 cm
1 foot = .305 m
1 yard = .914 m
1 mile = 1.61 km
1 fluid ounce = 29.573 ml
1 dry ounce = 28.35 g
1 pound = 0.45 kg
1 cup = .24 l
1 pint = .473 l
1 teaspoon = 4.93 ml

Conversion from Fahrenheit to Celsius: subtract 32 and then multiply the remainder by $\frac{5}{9}$.

ISBN: 0-8167-3190-X

Printed in the United States of America.

10 9 8 7 6 5 4 3

Contents

INTRODUCTION

Dear Teacher,

Autumn is approaching and that means many things: the excitement of a brand-new school year, holidays to celebrate, and changes in the weather. For teachers, autumn can often be the busiest time of the year. The classroom needs to be arranged and decorated, favorite items and games are brought out of the closet and dusted off, depleted materials need restocking, lesson plans must be reviewed and updated, and new students are ready and eager to learn.

As a teacher myself, I know that feeling of anticipation as September approaches. I have found that the more ideas and projects I gather before introducing a subject, the smoother my lesson plans go. I like idea books that are practical and do not call for a trip to a supply store for various materials. My favorite books include clearly written, grade-appropriate activities and ideas, and best of all, contain projects spanning several months and covering a variety of subjects. I treasure these books and return to them for inspiration year after year.

With this in mind, I've compiled some of my favorite and most useful activities, which I share with you here. The variety of projects, centered around a fall theme, will interest both you and your students. Cooperative learning and whole language approaches will enhance your class's appreciation of the season. And plenty of background information and teacher guidelines provide the perfect seasonal resource for primary classrooms.

Most of the activities here can be completed in just one classroom session. The easy-to-follow directions are illustrated as clearly as possible so that you will not have to stop a project while you try for the fifth time to glue craft sticks together in a seemingly impossible fashion, or figure out just when the sugar is supposed to be added to a recipe. And I've tried to limit the materials used to those that are easy to obtain and inexpensive.

Have fun with these activities, and I wish you the best of everything throughout the fall season!

Denise Bieniek, M.Ed.

Weather Chart

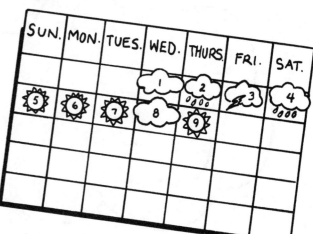

Materials:
- 20" x 22" sheet of light-colored oaktag
- yardstick
- crayons and markers
- scissors
- storage bag or file-folder
- thumbtacks

Directions:

1. Divide the oaktag into seven columns and six rows using a yardstick and a marker. Write the days of the week across the top boxes.

2. Reproduce the weather symbols ten times. Have a group of volunteers color the symbols and cut them out. Place the symbols in a storage bag or a file-folder for easy access.

3. Each day allow students time to look out the window or take a short walk outside to observe the weather.

4. Discuss the type of weather each day. Then have one or two students choose the matching weather symbol and write the date on it.

5. Tack the symbol to the oaktag sheet in the appropriate space to match those on the calendar. For example, if the date is Wednesday, the fifth of October, the student would tack the weather symbol to the Wednesday space on the weather chart.

6. After a month has gone by, ask the children what types of weather were most prevalent for that time period. Graph the weather on a bar graph with the class so they may see the information more clearly.

7. Ask the children to predict the weather for the next week based on the data they have already collected. At the end of the week compare the actual results with their predictions. Have students explain why their predictions were correct or incorrect.

8. For older children, ask students to collect the weather pages from the local newspaper for the same time period and compare their predictions to the actual weather.

Homework Helper

Directions:

1. Reproduce the homework helper pattern four times for each child. Have students color the sheets.

2. Explain to the class that each day they should write their homework assignments on these sheets and keep them in their folders or notebooks. This way, all their homework will be listed in one place.

3. If desired, ask each child to have a parent sign his or her initials next to each night's homework assignments after reviewing the child's work.

4. Homework helpers may be handed out at the start of each week, or on an as-needed basis.

Name _____

Date _____

Homework

_____

_____

_____

_____

_____

_____

_____

Birthday Bulletin Board

Materials:
- ◆ crayons or markers
- ◆ scissors
- ◆ birthday wrapping paper
- ◆ stapler
- ◆ glue

Directions:

1. Reproduce the cupcake pattern twelve times and the candle pattern once for each child. Color the cupcakes and write the name of one month of the year on each.

2. Distribute one candle per child and have each child color the candle and cut it out. Ask the children to write their names and birth dates on the candles sideways in black crayon or marker.

3. Glue each child's candle to the top of the appropriate cupcake in chronological order.

4. Cover a section of a bulletin board or a large display area with birthday wrapping paper. Then staple or glue the cupcakes to the board in rows so that students may read the names of the months in order.

5. Read the chart with students and review it at the start of each month to see which children will be celebrating birthdays that month. For summer birthdays, coordinate a class celebration at the end of the school year.

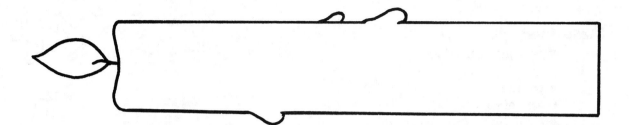

Job Chart

Materials:

- ◆ crayons or markers
- ◆ glue
- ◆ oaktag
- ◆ scissors
- ◆ clear contact paper
- ◆ white or light-colored bulletin board paper
- ◆ stick-on Velcro tabs
- ◆ stapler

Directions:

1. Reproduce the dinosaur figure once for each child. Reproduce the volcano pattern as many times as there are student jobs in the classroom. Have children color their dinosaurs, then mount the figures on oaktag and cut them out.

2. Ask children to write their names on the dinosaurs. Write the name of one classroom job on the base of each volcano.

3. Laminate both the dinosaurs and the volcanos.

4. Cover the job chart area with white or light-colored bulletin board paper. Staple or glue the volcanos in an up-and-down row as shown. Leave approximately 5" between volcanos.

5. Put a small Velcro tab on the back of each dinosaur and on the edge of each volcano. (Use two tabs if the job requires two children.)

6. Distribute the jobs each morning before the children arrive in the classroom by attaching a dinosaur to each tab. Be sure to vary the names on each volcano so that each child takes regular turns for each job. Go over the job chart with children at the start of each day.

Attendance Chart

Directions:

1. To make an attendance chart, make the dinosaurs and volcanos as in Step 1. Have each child write his or her name on a dinosaur. Then glue the dinosaurs to a large sheet of light-colored oaktag in random places.

2. Attach a small Velcro tab on the mouth of each dinosaur. Cut small leaves from green oaktag and attach a small Velcro tab on the back of those as well.

3. Each morning, have each child present attach a leaf in the mouth of the dinosaur showing his or her name. Then read the chart with the class to discover how many children are present and how many are absent.

4. Store the leaves in a bag attached to the attendance chart. After school each day, remove the leaves and place them back in the bag.

Getting to Know You

Materials:
- ◆ different-colored construction paper
- ◆ crayons and markers
- ◆ scissors
- ◆ collage materials and/or stickers
- ◆ hole punchers
- ◆ yarn

Directions:

1. Distribute construction paper to the class and ask each child to create his or her own name label. Give the children various collage materials to use to make their designs. Make sure children remember to write their names clearly.

2. Punch a hole on either side of the top of each label. Thread yarn through the holes and tie to make a necklace.

3. Divide the class into pairs. Try to match each child up with a classmate he or she does not know well. Ask the pairs to sit together to "interview" one another. Tell the children that they must find out the names of their partners, and a few pieces of information about them.

4. After several minutes, have children switch roles with their partners. When all the interviews are complete, have the class gather together in a circle.

5. Starting with the child seated on your left, ask each student to tell the name of his or her partner, and what he or she has learned about that classmate. Continue clockwise around the circle until everyone has had a turn.

6. When all the students have been introduced, ask if anyone can remember the names of everyone in the circle. Have volunteers walk around the outside of the circle trying to name each child.

7. Afterwards, create a word search worksheet using the names of the children in the class. Reproduce the worksheet and distribute it to children as a way of reinforcing classmates' names.

A	N	N	M	X	S	T	E	V	E
M	C	Y	U	K	U	E	V	J	R
Y	H	C	A	S	E	Y	A	G	I
B	O	B	B	Y	Q	H	N	L	N
O	U	Z	P	D	S	O	J	P	H
G	T	A	N	E	A	L	B	O	O
M	A	R	K	G	I	O	W	E	N

Scrambled Eggs Name Game

Directions:
1. Have children sit at their normally assigned places for this game, or arrange the children in rows on the floor.
2. Choose one child to be the leader. Have that child study the arrangement of the class, then go out of the room for one minute.
3. Select two children to switch seats before the leader returns. Then ask the leader to try to name which children have switched seats.
4. Give the leader two chances to answer correctly. Then have the leader choose another child to be the leader. Continue playing until everyone has had a turn.
5. For an additional challenge, have four children switch seats, or make no change at all.

Who Said That?

Directions:
1. Have children sit in a group on the floor or in chairs. Choose one child to be the first player.
2. The first player will come in front of the group and face away from them with eyes closed.
3. Choose another child to say a phrase or word in his or her own voice or in a disguised voice.
4. The first player gets three tries to name the child who spoke. If incorrect, the class may tell the speaker's name. Whether correct or incorrect, the speaker is the next player and the first child sits in his or her place with the group.

Name _____

Months of the Year

Cut apart each month along the lines. Then glue the months in order on a large piece of construction paper.

SEPTEMBER	JULY	APRIL
JANUARY	OCTOBER	JUNE
AUGUST	MAY	FEBRUARY
NOVEMBER	DECEMBER	MARCH

I Pledge Allegiance

Fill in the missing words to complete the Pledge of Allegiance.

I _____ allegiance to

the _____ of the

United States of _____

and to the republic for which it

_____ , one nation under

God, indivisible, with

_____ and justice for

_____ .

all   America

flag   stands

pledge   liberty

My Mini-Book About Me

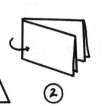

Materials:
- ◆ 11" x 17" photocopier paper
- ◆ crayons/markers

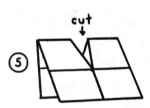

Directions:
1. Let children create their own mini-books about themselves during the first week of school. Begin by making a blank book for each child to fill in.

2. Fold the paper in half lengthwise. Then fold the paper in half widthwise two times as shown.

3. Unfold the paper to reveal eight sections. Write a cover title and fill-ins such as those suggested below on each section. Be sure to write in the direction shown below for each section.

4. Reproduce the completed paper once for each child. Fold each piece of paper in half widthwise, with the cover on the upper right as shown.

5. Cut the paper as shown from the top folded edge down to the top of the next section.

6. Open the paper flat. Fold each paper in half lengthwise as shown, with the cover in the back. Make folds for the unfolded sections on the far right and far left.

7. Push the ends together so that the middle opens into a diamond. Continue pushing until the diamond is closed flat. Then push the diamond down and fold the paper to complete the mini-book.

8. Give one book to each child. Help children fill in the books, and encourage them to draw pictures to illustrate each page.

9. Read each book aloud so that children become more familiar with each other. Then place the books on a table in the reading center for all to enjoy. After several weeks, return the books to the children for them to take home and share with their families.

NOTE: For older children, you may wish to demonstrate how to completely create their own books using light-colored construction paper.

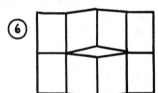

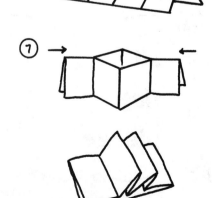

I like to ＿	I love ＿	My favorite animal is ＿	My favorite color is ＿ My favorite toy is ＿
The End	My Mini - Book About Me	My name is ＿	My birthday is ＿. I am ＿ years old.

Make Your Own Smocks

Materials:
- ◆ old button-down shirts (adult size)
- ◆ fabric paint and paintbrushes
- ◆ embroidery thread and needles
- ◆ buttons

Directions:

1. Ask each child to bring in an old adult button-down shirt from home to use as a smock. Request that the shirts be solid-colored.

2. Let children use fabric paint to write their names on their shirts. Children may also wish to draw pictures, designs, and patterns on their shirts.

3. Provide older children with embroidery thread, buttons, or other materials that may be sewn onto their clothes. Help children make sure the stitches and materials are secure enough to withstand machine washing.

4. When all the smocks have been completed, surprise the art teacher by having children wear their smocks to art class.

Back to School Reading Center

Create a quiet, comfortable environment for children to use as a reading center. Place bookcases and tables in a corner of the room to partition off a small area. Use an old rug to help distinguish the reading center from the rest of the classroom. Place large pillows, beanbag chairs, or soft, child-sized furniture in the reading center to make it even more cozy. Have a display table for class books and other creative writing projects. Create a book pattern and make mobiles or borders for decorations. Then make a sign for the wall that says, "Ssssh! Readers at Work!" or "Settle Down with a Good Book!"

Best Books for Back to School

◆ *Hello, Amigos!* written by Tricia Brown (Holt, 1986)

◆ *The Art Lesson*, written by Tomie dePaola (Putnam, 1989)

◆ *First Day of School*, written by Kim Jackson (Troll, 1985)

◆ *Second-Grade Dog*, written by Laurie Lawlor (Whitman, 1990)

◆ *The Cut-Ups Cut Loose*, written by James Marshall (Viking, 1987)

◆ *Teeny Witch Goes to School*, written by Liz Matthews (Troll, 1991)

◆ *Junie B. Jones and the Stupid Smelly Bus*, written by Barbara Park (Random House, 1992)

◆ *Annabelle Swift, Kindergartner*, written by Amy Schwartz (Orchard, 1988)

◆ *That Dreadful Day*, written by James Stevenson (Greenwillow, 1985)

Community Helpers

To help children learn more about their school and how it functions, take the class on a trip around the school. Make appointments with various school workers to ensure their availability. Once children are familiar with the workings of their school, branch out to local workers who perform neighborhood jobs, such as sanitation workers, mail carriers, police officers, firefighters, shop owners, and supermarket workers.

Directions:

1. Take the class to meet the school workers with whom they should be familiar: the principal, office workers, custodians, nurse, and to rooms they should know how to get to: office, custodian's office, nurse's office, gym, lunchroom, auditorium, library.

2. Help children prepare questions for the school workers. Include the following questions in your interviews:

- ◆ What is the name of the job you perform?
- ◆ What do you do in your job?
- ◆ Why or how did you choose your job?
- ◆ What can students do to help you in your job?

3. Make a display area with the interviews written up and taped to the display. Ask children to draw pictures of the workers doing their jobs and tape these to the display as well.

4. Ask the class to create ribbons or awards for the school workers to show their appreciation for all they do for the school.

5. Children may then discover the jobs of workers in their neighborhood. Follow the same steps as for school workers. Make up a list of workers to interview with the class and include those that are most important to the community and its smooth operation.

Name _____

O Canada!

Canada is the second-largest country in the world. The first European explorer to discover Canada was an Italian explorer named John Cabot in 1497. Although people from many different countries came to live in Canada, the early settlers were mostly made up of colonists from France and England. Today Canada has two official languages–French and English.

Canada is made up of ten provinces and two territories. On September 1, 1905, two new western provinces, Alberta and Saskatchewan, were created.

Solve the equations below to figure out the names of each province or territory. Then write each name in its place on the map.

Provinces

18 — 8 = Ontario	16 + 5 = Nova Scotia
8 + 12 = Quebec	17 + 8 = Alberta
17 — 9 = Newfoundland	15 — 9 = Saskatchewan
12 + 4 = New Brunswick	9 + 9 = Manitoba
19 — 5 = Prince Edward Island	13 + 13 = British Columbia

Territories

20 — 7 = Yukon Territory	13 — 4 = Northwest Territories

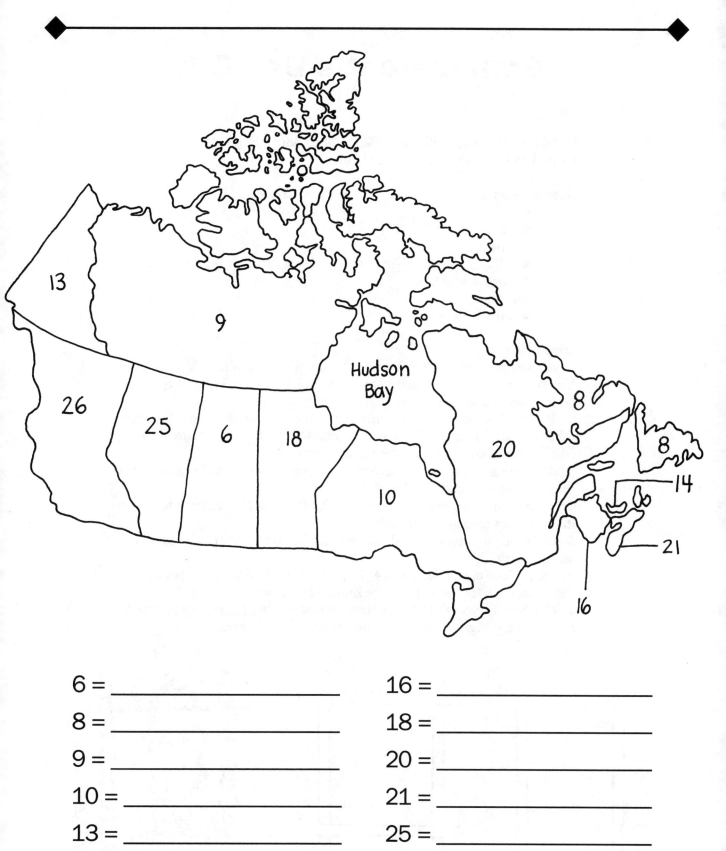

6 = _____   16 = _____

8 = _____   18 = _____

9 = _____   20 = _____

10 = _____   21 = _____

13 = _____   25 = _____

14 = _____   26 = _____

Grandparent's Day Gift

Celebrate Grandparent's Day (the first Sunday in September after Labor Day) by making this special gift.

Materials:
- ◆ craft sticks
- ◆ wax paper
- ◆ glue
- ◆ collage materials (small shells, beads, flowers, lace, cutouts)
- ◆ camera and film
- ◆ scissors
- ◆ narrow ribbon

Directions:
1. Give each child four craft sticks. In small groups, show the children how to arrange the craft sticks to make a picture frame. Begin by laying two sticks on wax paper side by side, about 4″ apart.

2. Put a dab of glue 1″ from each end of the craft sticks. Then lay the other two sticks across the first two, also 4″ apart, making sure their edges extend beyond the first pair, as shown.

3. After the glue has dried, have the children decorate the fronts of their frames with collage materials.

4. Take a close-up photograph of each child, or ask the children to bring in pictures of themselves from home.

5. Glue each photograph to the back of its frame, trimming the excess as necessary.

6. Glue a loop of ribbon, about 4″ long, to the back of the craft stick at the top of each frame so it may be hung on a hook.

7. Children may wish to create their own wrapping paper for the gifts by drawing designs on construction paper or tissue paper.

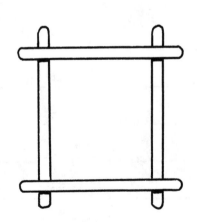

Grandparent's Day Greeting Card

Materials:
- ◆ crayons and markers
- ◆ scissors

Directions:

1. Reproduce the piano and top on page 28 once for each child. Have the children color the cards and cut them out.

2. Demonstrate how to glue along the top of the piano where the cover is missing from the strings. Lay the piano top over the strings so it covers them completely and looks like the piano is closed. Let dry.

3. Children may write the name(s) of the card's recipient(s) on the cover. Inside they may write special messages, such as, "You're the grandest of them all!" before signing their names.

4. Tell children to attach the cards to the Grandparent's Day Gift.

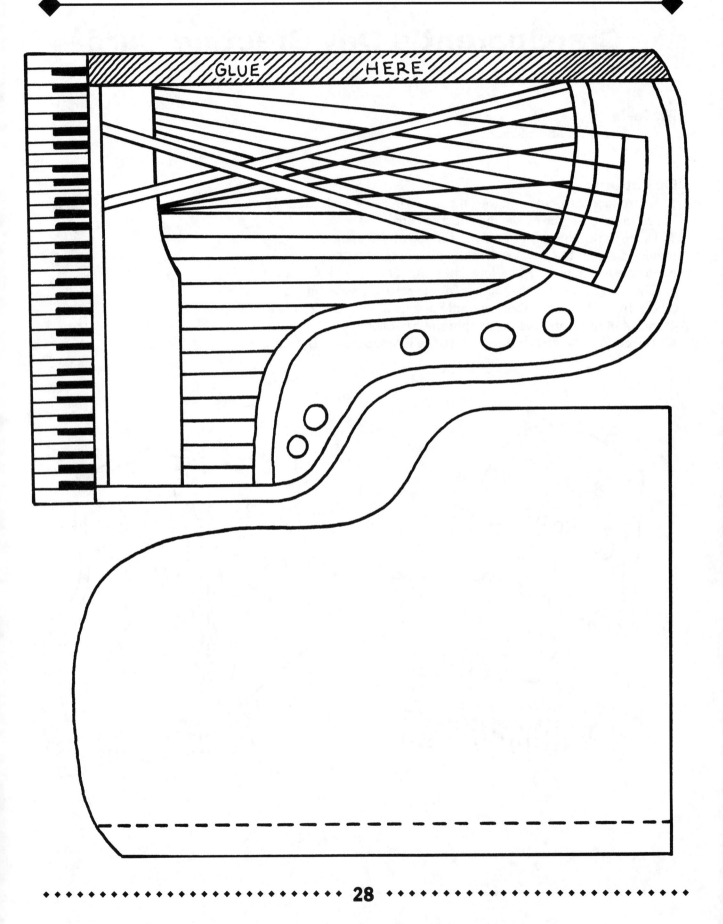

Grandparent's Interview

As a Grandparent's Day activity, ask each student to "interview" a grandparent, older relative, or friend about what life was like when they were young. Have a class discussion to come up with questions for students to ask. Some suggested questions are:

1. What kind of school did you go to? How did you get to school each day? Did you go on field trips? What kinds of things did you like to do in school?

2. How many brothers and sisters do you have? Did you fight with them when you were growing up? What jobs did your parents have? Did you go on family trips or vacations?

3. What foods did you eat for breakfast, lunch, dinner, and snack? Who prepared the meals in your house? What was your favorite food and drink? Did you ever go out to a restaurant?

4. What games did you play with your friends? What was your favorite indoor game? What was your favorite outdoor game? Did you like to read? What was your favorite book? Did you borrow books from a town library or school library? Did you buy books in a bookstore?

5. What songs and movies were popular when you were young? Do you like those songs and movies better than the ones today?

Have children make cassette tape recordings of their interviews, or write up highlights from their interviews. When all the interviews have been completed, let children share their interviews with the rest of the class.

Family Tree Big Book

Materials:
- ◆ 12" x 18" construction paper
- ◆ crayons or markers
- ◆ hole puncher
- ◆ yarn

Directions:
1. Give each child several sheets of light-colored construction paper. Draw a family tree on a chalkboard as shown. Help children make their own family trees on the construction paper with the appropriate number of leaves to fit their families.

2. Have children fill in the leaves on their trees with the names of their family members.

3. Ask children to choose several members of their families to feature on separate pieces of paper. Have each child draw pictures of the selected family members, or show scenes of him or herself doing a favorite activity with each person.

4. Let children make covers for their books and title them. Have children arrange the pages in order and punch two holes along the left side. Tie yarn through the holes to bind the books.

5. Have the class gather together in a circle to share their books. After all the books have been presented, discuss various types of families (traditional, single-parent, combined, etc.) and how family units differ all over the country and the world.

Best Books About Grandparents

◆ *Song and Dance Man*, written by Karen Ackerman (Knopf, 1988)

◆ *Now One Foot, Now the Other*, written by Tomie dePaola (Putnam, 1981)

◆ *A Balloon for Grandad*, written by Nigel Gray (Orchard, 1988)

◆ *Georgia Music*, written by Helen V. Griffith (Greenwillow, 1986)

◆ *Grandaddy's Place*, written by Helen V. Griffith (Greenwillow, 1987)

◆ *Katie Morag and the Two Grandmothers*, written by Mairi Hedderwick (Little, Brown, 1986)

◆ *Grandpa and Bo*, written by Kevin Henkes (Greenwillow, 1986)

◆ *The Purple Coat*, written by Amy Hest (Four Winds, 1986)

◆ *The Grandma Mix-Up*, written by Emily Arnold McCully (HarperCollins, 1988)

◆ *Grandmas at the Lake*, written by Emily Arnold McCully (HarperCollins, 1990)

Name _____

Spanish Colors

Mexico Independence Day is celebrated on September 16. Use the key at the bottom of the page to translate the Spanish words. Then color in the picture.

1	**amarillo**	**5**	**pardo**
2	**azul**	**6**	**anaranjado**
3	**rojo**	**7**	**blanco**
4	**verde**	**8**	**negro**

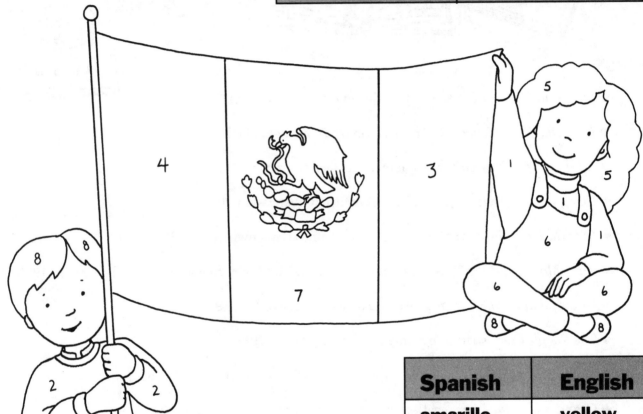

Spanish	English
amarillo	**yellow**
azul	**blue**
rojo	**red**
verde	**green**
pardo	**brown**
anaranjado	**orange**
blanco	**white**
negro	**black**

Name _____

Happy New Year!

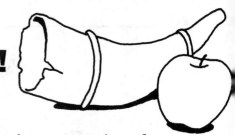

The Jewish New Year is called Rosh Hashanah. It is a very important day of remembrance when Jewish people think about the things they have done during the past year. People express remorse for the things they have done wrong and any sadness they might have caused.

Rosh Hashanah falls during the month of September or October. On this holy day Jewish families go to temple and say prayers. People are called to gather in their synagogues by the sound of a shofar, which is a trumpet made from the horn of a ram. Afterwards, everyone celebrates with a special dinner that includes challah bread, gefilte fish, and apples with honey, which symbolize good luck.

1. What is the name of the Jewish New Year?

   _____

2. Where do people go to pray on this day?

   _____

3. What is the name of the trumpet that is blown?

   _____

4. What does the trumpet remind people to do?

   _____

5. How do people celebrate after they go to temple?

   _____

6. What kinds of food do people eat on Rosh Hashanah?

   _____

◆ ◆

Apple Observations

Use apples to help children develop their observation skills.

Directions:

1. Ask each child to bring in one apple. Tell the children to observe their apples carefully, noting as many details as they can. Then ask each student to use a washable marker to write his or her initials on the bottom of the apple and place it on a table.

2. Give children a sheet of paper and a pencil. Ask them questions about their apples and have them write the answers on their papers. Some suggested questions are:

◆ What color(s) is your apple?
◆ Does it have a stem?
◆ Are there any bruises or bumps on your apple?
◆ How big is your apple?

3. Survey the class to find out how many knew all the answers. Then have two volunteers come to the table and categorize the apples. The students may wish to sort by color, size, stem or no stem, or by other means. After the apples have been sorted, have the rest of the class guess by which criteria the children are sorting.

4. Have children come to the table to see if they can find their own apples without looking at the marks on the bottoms.

5. Ask children to wash their apples well. Then distribute plastic knives to children and tell them they will be cutting open their apples from stem to bottom. Before they do, have them draw a picture of what they think the apple will look like inside. Also, have children estimate how many seeds they think are inside their apples before cutting them open.

6. Have each child count the seeds inside his or her apple. Graph the results on a bar graph. If desired, make a second graph categorizing each type of apple (Granny Smith, McIntosh, Rome Beauty) and the number of seeds found in them.

7. Children may wish to taste the different types of apples, then plant the seeds.

Apple Cake Recipe

Materials:
- 2 cups flour
- 1 teaspoon baking soda
- 1 teaspoon cinnamon
- 1/2 teaspoon salt
- 3 eggs
- 1 3/4 cups sugar
- 1 cup vegetable oil
- 4-5 skinned apples
- plastic knives
- mixing bowls
- wooden spoons
- 11″ × 15″ baking pan

Servings: approximately 18

Directions:
1. Give a group of four children plastic knives and instruct them to cut the apples into small cubes.
2. Have another group measure the dry ingredients and mix them together in a small bowl.
3. Give a third group the eggs and sugar to beat together until well blended in a large bowl. Then add the oil and beat again.
4. Stir in the dry ingredients until moist. Fold in apple cubes.
5. Pour the batter into a greased 11″ × 15″ baking pan and bake in a 350°F oven for 45 minutes. Let cool, then cut into approximately 18 squares.

Frozen Apple Juice Ice Pops

Materials:
- permanent marker
- 6 oz. plastic cups
- apple juice
- craft sticks
- tape

Directions:
1. Show children how to write their names on their cups in permanent marker. Have children fill their cups halfway with apple juice.
2. Tell each child to insert a craft stick into the juice. Show each child how to use tape to hold the craft stick in place in the middle of the juice.
3. Before placing the cups in the freezer, discuss the properties of the juice as a liquid. After the juice has frozen, discuss the changes that have taken place.
4. Have children remove the tape from the craft stick. Then show children how to carefully squeeze the frozen juice pop from the bottom of the cup. Enjoy!

Apple Fractions

Directions:
1. Ask each child to bring in an apple from home. Divide the class into four groups. Have one group cut their apples in half, another group in thirds, and a third group in fourths. Ask the fourth group to leave their apples intact.
2. Give each group paper to write the fraction their apples represent. Place the papers on a table next to the apples.
3. Allow children time to view the apples and observe the different sizes of each fraction. When all are seated again, have one child from each group come up with one of the apple pieces.
4. Ask volunteers to put the apples in size order from largest to smallest and smallest to largest.
5. Let children make an accordion book to help them remember fraction sizes. Distribute two sheets of 8 1/2" x 11" photocopier paper to each child. Demonstrate how to fold both sheets in half lengthwise.
6. Then help children tape the two sheets together to form one long accordion booklet. Make sure the cover page opens to the left as shown.
7. Reproduce the apple patterns on page 37. Have each child glue the whole apple to the first page, the half apple to the second page, the apple in thirds to the third page, and the apple in fourths to the last page. Tell the children to write the fraction name for each apple (whole, halves, thirds, fourths) underneath its picture.

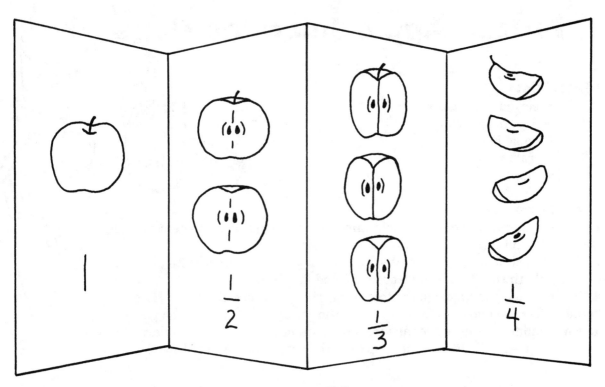

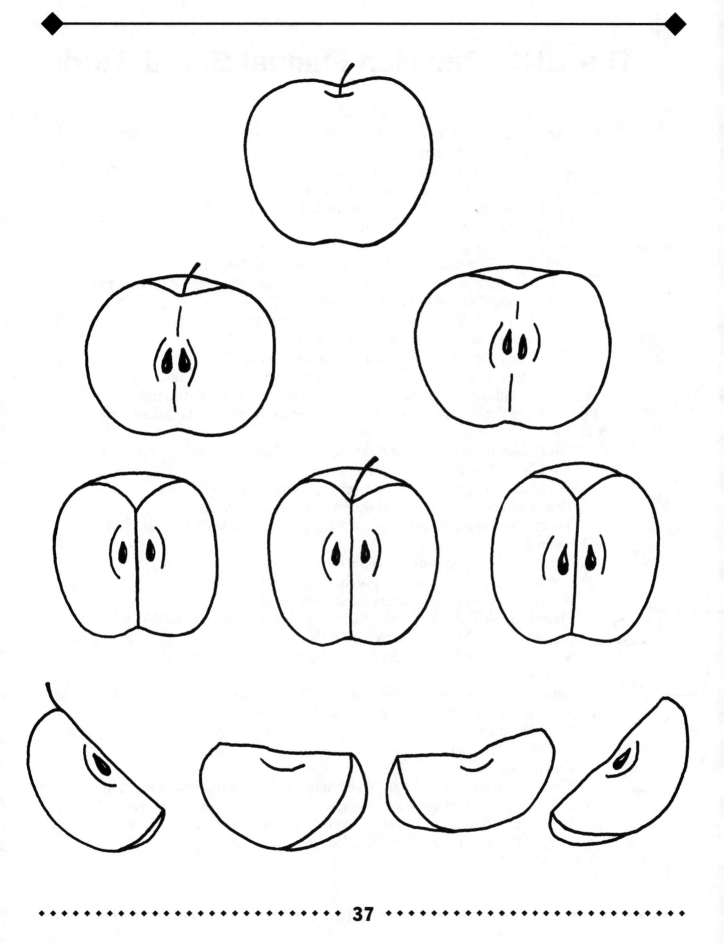

The Little Red Hen Flannel Board Story

Long, long ago there lived a little red hen. She worked on her farm with a dog, a cat, and a pig.

One day the little red hen decided to plant some grains of wheat. "Who will help me plant the wheat?" she asked her friends.

"Not I," said the dog, who was playing ball.

"Not I," said the cat, who was taking a nap.

"Not I," said the pig, who was rolling in mud.

"Then I will do it myself," said the little red hen. And she did.

Soon the golden wheat grew tall and was ready to be cut. "Who will help me cut the wheat?" asked the little red hen.

"Not I," said the dog, who was tired from running.

"Not I," said the cat, who was chasing a bird.

"Not I," said the pig, who was drinking some water.

"Then I will do it myself," said the little red hen. And she did.

After she cut the wheat, the little red hen needed to take it to the mill to be ground into flour. "Who will take the wheat to the mill?" she asked her friends.

"Not I," said the dog, who was resting in the sun.

"Not I," said the cat, who was licking her paw.

"Not I," said the pig, who was watching the grass grow.

"Then I will do it myself," said the little red hen. And she did.

The little red hen decided to use the flour to make a loaf of bread. "Who will help me bake the bread?"

"Not I," said the dog, who was chasing a squirrel.

"Not I," said the cat, who was playing with a ball of yarn.

"Not I," said the pig, who was eating some swill.

"Then I will do it myself," said the little red hen. And she did.

In a short time the bread came out of the oven. The little red hen placed it on a windowsill to cool. A wonderful smell drifted over to where the dog, the cat, and the pig were playing.

The little red hen came to the window. "Hello," she said to her friends. "I was just wondering, who will help me eat this bread?"

"I will!" said the dog.

"I will!" said the cat.

"I will!" said the pig.

"Now, let me see," said the little red hen. "I planted the wheat and tended to it all by myself. Then I cut the wheat and took it to the mill to be ground into flour all by myself. And I used the flour to bake this beautiful bread all by myself as well. So now I shall eat this loaf of bread—all by myself."

And she did.

The Little Red Hen Flannel Board

Reproduce each of the figures below and on page 40. Color the figures and cut them out. Glue flannel to the backs of the figures and let children move them around a flannel board as they hear the story.

The Little Red Hen Flannel Board

Name _____

Fire Safety Secret Message

Fire Prevention Week is the second week of October. Decode these fire safety messages to earn your firefighter's badge. Write the first letter of each picture and solve the equations on the lines provided.

Fire Safety Badge

Directions:

1. Reproduce the safety badge once for each child in the class.
2. Mount each badge on oaktag and cut out.
3. Write the child's name on the line provided.
4. Punch a hole at the top of the badge. Thread a 24" length of yarn through the hole and tie.

The Voyage of Columbus

Materials:
- ◆ crayons and markers
- ◆ scissors
- ◆ glue
- ◆ 12" x 18" light blue construction paper

Directions:
1. Reproduce the shapes on this page many times. Distribute a certain number to each table. Tell the children that they will be making a picture of Christopher Columbus's journey across the sea using only the shapes on the papers.
2. Have the children color and cut out the shapes, then glue them to light blue construction paper to create scenes involving Columbus and his crew on their journey.
3. If desired, students may create smaller versions of the shapes on this page.
4. Have each child write a short story describing his or her picture.
5. When all the pictures have been completed, ask the children to share their pictures and stories of Columbus with the class.

Name _____

Float or Sink?

Which things in this picture will sink in water and which things will float? Write an "S" on the objects that sink and an "F" on the objects that float.

Float or Sink Experiments

1. Divide the class into groups of four. Give students a variety of small classroom objects (such as paper clips, sponges, rubber bands, paper scraps, and fabric scraps) to use for their experiments.

2. Ask students to predict which objects will float and which will sink before they place them in the water. Then give the groups time to explore the properties of each object and its ability or inability to float.

3. When the groups have tested each object, ask them to gather together and discuss the results of their findings. Then ask the children to make predictions about other objects found outside the classroom. Try to explain in simple terms that some objects are more dense than water, and some are less dense. Things that are less dense float; things that are more dense sink.

4. Draw a tub of water on a large sheet of oaktag. Ask one person from each group to tape something that floated on the surface of the water. Then have someone from each group tape an object that sank to the bottom of the tub. Continue until all objects tested have been attached to the oaktag.

Columbus Hat

Materials:
- newspapers
- masking tape
- paint and paintbrushes
- collage materials
- glue

Directions:

1. Display books containing color pictures from Christopher Columbus's time. Discuss the fashions of the time with the class, such as colors, length of dresses and skirts, pants and jackets for men, children's clothing, shoe styles, and hat styles.

2. Tell the children that they will be making a hat like the one Columbus wore on his journey. Have each child draw a sketch of how he or she thinks the hat will look.

3. Give each child three sheets of newspaper. Lay the newspaper on the child's head and wrap it around the head down to the child's forehead. Have the child hold the newspaper in place.

4. Wrap masking tape on the newspaper around the child's head just above the eyebrows. Be sure not to tape it too tightly. Place a mirror before the child and have him or her roll the excess as desired. For example, some children may wish to roll the excess along the front up to the masking tape band and leave the back hanging long. Others may wish to roll the excess all the way around. After the child has rolled the newspaper, secure the hat with masking tape.

5. Let the children paint their hats any color they wish. After the paint is dry, lay out trays of collage materials, including feathers, beads, sequins, paper cutouts, yarn, lace, and fabric scraps. Have students personalize their hats with decorative touches.

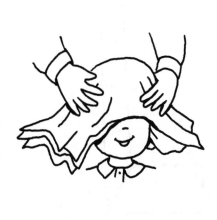

Name _____

Take a Trip with Columbus

What kinds of things did Christopher Columbus and his crew take with them on their voyage from Spain? What kinds of things would they take with them on their voyage if they went today? Cut apart the objects at the bottom of the page. Then paste each object inside the proper trunk.

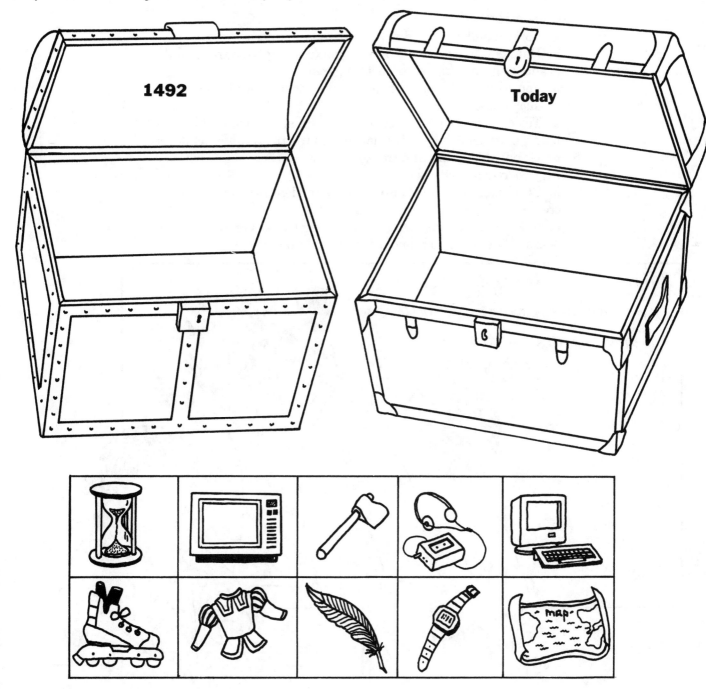

Autumn Tree Bulletin Board

Materials:
- light yellow bulletin board paper
- brown construction paper
- yellow, red, orange, and green fingerpaint
- shallow pans

Directions:
1. Cover a bulletin board with light yellow paper.
2. Have children work together to make a large tree trunk and branches from brown construction paper.
3. Pour yellow, red, orange, and green fingerpaint into separate shallow pans.
4. Tell children to place their hands palm-side down in the fingerpaint, then make handprint "leaves" on the tree. Advise children to use one color paint at a time, and to wash their hands when they wish to switch colors.
5. Children may wish to superimpose the leaves on each other to create a collage of fall colors on the tree.
6. If desired, copy the poem below in large letters on the bulletin board. Title the bulletin board "Autumn Colors."

Yellow, red, orange, green.
Can you guess what I've just seen?
Autumn colors in the air,
Autumn colors everywhere!

Stained Glass Leaves

Materials:

- ◆ scissors
- ◆ oaktag
- ◆ black construction paper
- ◆ cellophane paper
- ◆ tape

Directions:

1. Reproduce the leaf patterns on page 50 once and cut them out.

2. Trace the patterns onto oaktag and cut them out. Then have each child trace an oaktag leaf onto black construction paper and cut it out.

3. Show children how to fold the leaves in half and cut out "veins" for the leaves.

4. Give children cellophane paper to glue to the backs of the leaves. Have children trim off the excess cellophane.

5. Tape the leaves to a classroom window to make a stained glass leaf display for everyone to enjoy.

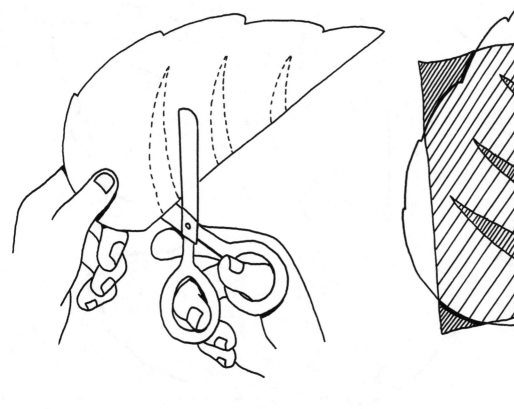

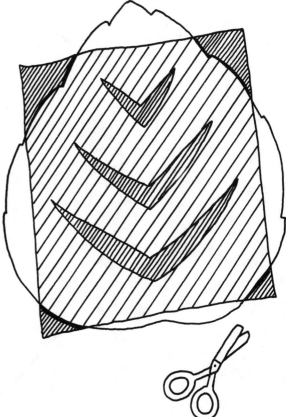

FOLD

FOLD

FOLD

FOLD

Seasons Science Experiment

Help children learn about day and night by doing the following experiment using a flashlight and a globe.

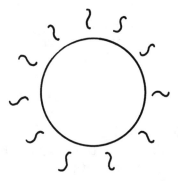

Directions:

1. Discuss what the words *day* and *night* mean to children. Talk about what the sky looks like during the day and at night. Ask the class what sorts of activities they do during the day and at night. Write their comments on experience chart paper.

2. Inform children that while it is day where they live, it is night on the other side of the world. Demonstrate this phenomenon with a flashlight and a globe. Choose one child to hold the flashlight and turn it on. This will be the "sun." Choose another child to stand a few feet away holding the globe. Let the rest of the class stand in a circle around the two.

3. Turn off the lights. Ask one child to point to the areas that are experiencing day. Then ask another to point to the areas that are experiencing night.

4. Ask the child with the globe to turn it very slowly so the day side becomes night and the night side becomes day. Now have two more children point out day and night.

5. Explain that the Earth, where we live, turns on its axis every 24 hours. The Earth is constantly moving; this is what makes day and night.

6. The Earth also moves around the sun. However, it is the Earth's tilted axis that causes the seasons. The part of the Earth that is closest to the sun has warm weather.

7. Choose two more children to hold the flashlight and globe. Point out how the Earth tilts at an angle. Have the child with the globe move around the "sun," keeping the tilt of the globe in the same direction. Ask the children to tell which season the Earth might be experiencing at these times.

Falling Thermometer!

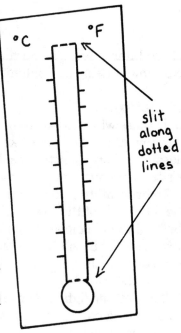

slit along dotted lines

Materials:
- ◆ crayons or markers
- ◆ glue
- ◆ oaktag
- ◆ clear contact paper
- ◆ scissors
- ◆ 8″ strips of red and white flannel
- ◆ different types of thermometers

Directions:
1. Reproduce the thermometer pattern. Color the thermometer and mount it on oaktag.

2. Laminate the oaktag and cut out the thermometer. Then cut two slits, one at either end of the thermometer's tube, as shown.

3. Glue one end of an 8" red flannel strip to one end of an 8" white flannel strip.

4. Insert the ends in the slits on the thermometer and glue the free ends together so the flannel is not too loose.

5. Explain to the class that thermometers tell people how hot or cold something is, such as the inside of an oven, or the air outside. Tell students that there are all types of thermometers. If possible, display various thermometers and explain their uses. (Some common thermometers are those for measuring fever, meat, and air.) Explain also that some thermometers measure temperature in Fahrenheit and some in Celsius.

6. Each morning, have children take a real thermometer outside and measure the air temperature. Record the temperature on a chart and move the red flannel strip so it resembles the temperature on the real thermometer. Repeat the process in the afternoon.

7. Compare the temperatures on a weekly and monthly basis. Discuss the temperature at the beginning of each week or month and then again at the end. Talk about any patterns children notice, such as a downward or upward trend in temperature, extreme variances, and constant temperatures.

8. Collect the weather pages from the local newspaper that show temperatures across the country and/or around the world. Have children try to find a country experiencing the same temperatures as they have had. Have them find a city with temperatures below or above those they have been having. Compare and contrast temperatures in the different regions across the country. Try to predict which city or country will have the same temperature as they will for the coming week or month.

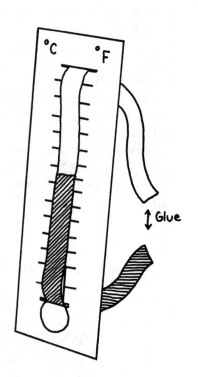

Glue

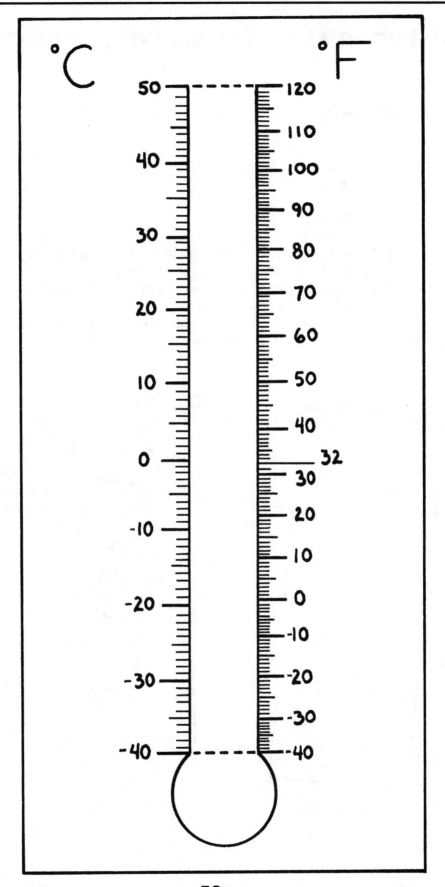

Autumn Doorknob Decorations

Materials:
- ◆ glue
- ◆ oaktag
- ◆ scissors
- ◆ crayons/markers

Directions:
1. Reproduce the doorknob decorations once for each child.
2. Have children glue the decorations onto oaktag and cut out.
3. Let children color and decorate their work.
4. Help children cut a slit on the right or left side of the door-knob holder, then cut out the center circle as shown.
5. Children may take home their doorknob decorations to use in their bedrooms or playrooms.

Harvest Time

Fall Fun

Nature Treasure Hunt

Plan an outdoor nature walk with the class. Create a treasure hunt for the children to make the trip fun for everyone by making up riddles to help the class move from one spot to another.

Begin the treasure hunt in the classroom, reading a riddle such as, "I am made of wood. In the autumn, leaves fall from my branches." Then tape a second riddle to a prominent tree in the school yard. Gear the difficulty level of the riddles to the age of the children in the class, and encourage children to work together to solve each riddle.

At the end of the treasure hunt, have a fall treat such as a basket of apples or a bowl of popcorn waiting for the children.

Before departing on the treasure hunt, discuss with the class the types of autumn things they think they might see on the walk. Write children's predictions on a chalkboard. When the class returns to the classroom, check off the objects that were observed on the trip. Ask volunteers to name other autumn things that were seen, and list them on the chalkboard as well.

Autumn Math

Discuss the importance of math with the class. Explain that math is used in everyday life in many different ways. Ask volunteers to give some examples of when they use their math skills. Tell children that people use math when they play sports and board games, when they shop for food, clothing, and other things, when they cook, when they drive, and many other times throughout the day.

Encourage children to find examples of how people use math during the autumn. Have each child draw a picture depicting an autumn activity that requires math skills, and write or dictate a sentence describing the particular skill that is used.

Name _____

Football Fun

Use the key provided to solve these football word problems. Begin on the 0 yard line. Write the answer to each question on the line provided.

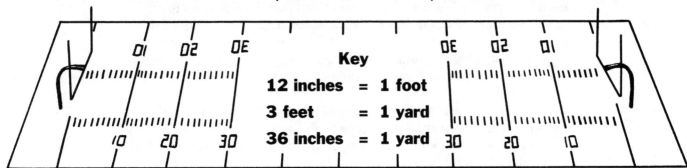

1. Take the ball and run 12 feet. Your ball is now on the _____ yard line.

2. Catch a pass and gain 17 yards. Now you're on the _____ yard line.

3. Rush through the middle and gain just 72 inches. This puts you on the _____ yard line.

4. A short pass gains you 6 yards. Your ball is now on the _____ yard line.

5. Hike! You grab the ball and run 60 feet. You're on the _____ yard line.

6. Fumble! You recover the ball, but you lose 360 inches. This puts you on the _____ yard line.

7. Another successful pass helps you gain 9 yards. Your ball is now on the _____ yard line.

8. You decide to try for a field goal. How many yards do you have to kick the ball? _____

Name _____

World Series Mystery

Someone has stolen some numbers from the World Series scoreboard! Read the clues below to fill in the missing numbers to show who has won the game.

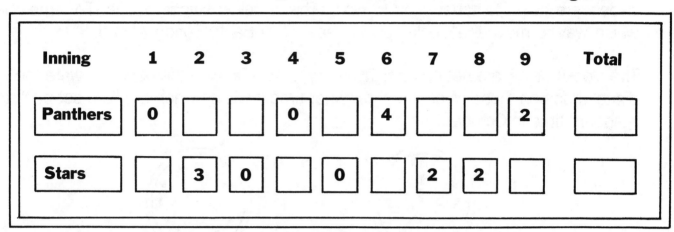

Inning	1	2	3	4	5	6	7	8	9	Total
Panthers	0			0		4			2	
Stars		3	0		0		2	2		

1. At the end of the first inning the game was tied.
2. At the end of the second inning the Panthers were losing by two runs.
3. At the end of the third inning the Panthers had tied the game again.
4. At the end of the fourth inning the Stars had taken a one-run lead.
5. At the end of the fifth inning the Panthers were losing by one run.
6. At the end of the sixth inning the Stars were losing by three runs.
7. At the end of the seventh inning the Panthers had a one-run lead.
8. At the end of the eighth inning the Stars were leading by one run.
9. The Stars and the Panthers scored the same amount of runs in the ninth inning.

Name _____

What Time Is It?

In the spring we set our clocks one hour ahead so that it stays light out longer in the evening. This is called daylight-saving time. Then in the fall, on the last Sunday in October, we set our clocks back one hour earlier so that the sun is up when people are going to school and to work. This is called standard time. To remember which way to move the clocks, people say, "Fall Back, Spring Ahead."

The clocks below are set on daylight saving time. Draw in the hands or write the digital times on these clocks to show what time it will be when they are set back to standard time in October.

Sundial Experiments

Tell students that in the days before people owned clocks and watches, they used to tell time by looking at the sun and the shadows it made. The shorter the shadow, the closer it was to noon; the longer the shadow, the closer it was to evening. However, this method was not very accurate because shadows are naturally longer in winter than in summer (due to the path the Earth travels around the sun), and this would disrupt their telling of time. For example, a shadow cast about 4:00 P.M. on a winter's day might resemble a shadow cast about 6:00 P.M. on a summer's day.

Long ago, people would place a stick in the ground. At noon, there would be the shortest shadow since the sun was directly overhead. People could tell approximately what time it was by looking at which side of the stick the shadow was and how long it was. Again, time was still not very accurate because the stick had to be exactly parallel to the Earth's axis, and this can really only be done at the North and South Poles.

Tell the class that they will try to estimate time just as people did long ago. Place a stick in a patch of dirt outside school. Try to make the stick stand as straight as possible. Observe the shadows of the stick in the morning, afternoon, and before leaving for the day. Try to find out when exact noon is according to the stick. (There should be only the barest of shadows because the sun will be directly overhead.) Then have students see if it matches exact noon according to the clock.

Children can mark off the hours by tracing the line on the ground cast by the shadow of the stick (beginning with noon) as each hour passes. Encourage students to see if the time is accurate from day to day.

Do You Have the Time? Card Game

Materials:
- ◆ glue
- ◆ oaktag
- ◆ scissors
- ◆ marker

Directions:
1. Reproduce the clock faces at the bottom of this page 24 times.
2. Mount the clock faces on oaktag and cut apart.
3. Write the analogue time of day on one game card, and the digital time for that same hour on another game card, as shown. Write the time for each hour and half hour, i.e., 12:00, 12:30, 1:00, 1:30, 2:00, 2:30, and so on. Continue until all 48 cards have been completed.
4. Shuffle the cards and spread them out facedown on a playing table. Then let two children at a time play a "Concentration"-type game.
5. The first player turns over any two cards. If the cards match, the player keeps the cards. If they do not match, the cards are turned back facedown in the same spots. Then the next player goes and turns over any two cards, and play continues.
6. Encourage players to try to remember where various cards are located. The game ends when all the cards have been matched. The player with the most matches wins.

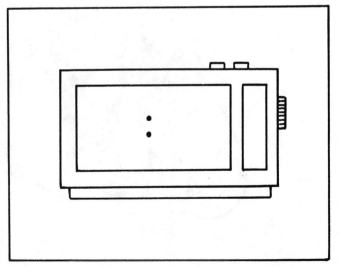

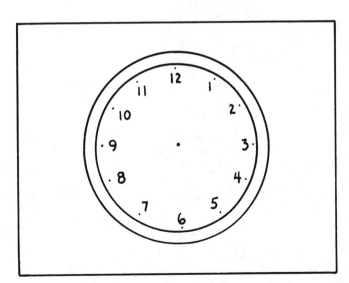

Shadow Art

1. Invite children outside on a sunny morning to an open area of a concrete play yard. Have children select partners.

2. Demonstrate how to use chalk to trace around a child's shadow while that child remains standing. Then have the pairs trace each other's shadows on the ground.

3. Discuss the length of the shadow and any other observations the children wish to make.

4. Bring the class back to the same spot in the afternoon. Have students stand in the same positions to be traced again.

5. Compare and contrast the shadows from the morning and those of the afternoon. Ask children to explain why they think the shadows are different (the position of the sun in the sky changes the shadows). What do they think will happen later in the day? What will happen very early in the morning?

6. Upon returning to the classroom, write children's comments on the chalkboard under the headings of "Morning Shadows" and "Afternoon Shadows." Conclude that in the morning, shadows are shorter, and in the afternoon, they are longer.

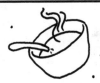 # Nail Soup

Once upon a time there was a man who wandered from town to town. Although he had nothing to his name, this man did possess a natural gift of charm, which often helped him get by.

One day the man came to a little house at the edge of a wood. He knocked on the door, hoping to be invited in for a nice meal.

An old woman answered the door. "Hello!" said the man. "I was wondering if you might let me warm myself by the fire, and perhaps have a bite to eat."

The old woman scowled. "I haven't got anything to eat," she said. "There isn't a morsel in the house. You'd best be going."

But the man was not easily persuaded. "You haven't a thing to eat!" he cried. "Well, then I shall share my fortune with you. Bring me a pot!"

Since the old woman was very curious as to what this vagabond intended to offer her, she fetched him a pot. The man filled the pot with some water and hung it over the fire. Then he carefully took a nail from his pocket and placed it in the pot.

"What exactly are you making?" the puzzled woman asked.

"Nail soup," said the man.

Now, the old woman had seen many things in her day, but she had never seen anyone make soup from a nail.

"This nail makes exceptionally fine broth," said the man. "Unfortunately, I have been using the same nail all week, so this batch will probably be a little thin. If only we had a cup or two of flour to add to it."

"I might have a bit of flour," said the woman. She hurried to her cupboard and gave the man the flour.

"This is wonderful," said the man, stirring in the flour. "Of course, a few potatoes could make a world of difference."

"Potatoes?" asked the woman. "I think I have one or two."

She fetched the potatoes and the man added them to the pot.

"Mmmmm," said the man, tasting the soup. "This is just about the finest nail soup I've ever made. The only thing that's missing is..."

"Some carrots and some milk?" asked the woman. And of course, she gave these to the man.

Finally the man declared that the soup was ready. He added some salt and pepper for seasoning, then poured the soup into two huge bowls. Before they sat down, the old woman took a loaf of bread from the cupboard and cut them each a big slice.

The old woman took a spoonful of soup. "My goodness!" she said. "This is the finest soup I have ever tasted!"

The man nodded his head in agreement. "And to think that all you need is a nail," he said with a smile.

Discussion Questions:

1. Why did the old woman tell the man that she didn't have any food in the house?
2. What do you think nail soup would taste like?
3. What do you think might have happened if the woman didn't add any food to the soup?
4. Why do you think the soup tasted so good to the old woman?
5. What kinds of things would you like to put in nail soup?
6. Have the class think up new endings to the story.

United Nations Day

On October 24, 1945, the United Nations was formed. This organization is made up of most of the countries in the world, joined together for a common goal of promoting peace and advancement for all nations.

The headquarters for the United Nations is located in New York City. The head of the United Nations is the secretary general. The secretary general conducts the business of the United Nations, and meets with the General Assembly. Every country that is a member of the United Nations sends a representative to the General Assembly to help decide what to do about world problems.

Over 150 countries are members of the United Nations. To decorate the classroom for United Nations Day, have children make flags for the different countries of the world. Provide children with reference books and decorating materials. See how many of the flags the class can complete. Hang the posters as a border along the classroom walls.

United Nations Day

Pumpkin Observations

Directions:

1. Have each child bring in a pumpkin of any size. On each group's table lay out paper clips, string, and any other non-standard units of measurement that might be appropriate. Ask the groups to measure how wide and how tall their pumpkins are using the objects on the table. Then have children share their findings.

2. Write the different lengths on a chalkboard next to each child's name. Compare whose pumpkin is the widest, narrowest, tallest, and shortest.

3. Discuss the outside of the pumpkins. How many sections does each child's pumpkin have? Do bigger pumpkins have more sections? Do smaller pumpkins have fewer sections? Is there a relationship between the sections and the stem?

4. Weigh the pumpkins. Ask students to predict which ones will weigh more and which ones will weigh less. What will happen to the weight of the pumpkins after the inside is emptied?

5. Before cutting open their pumpkins, ask students if they think there might be a relationship between the sections on the outside of a pumpkin and its interior structure. Have children predict how many seeds they think are in their pumpkins. Do bigger pumpkins have more seeds than smaller pumpkins?

6. Help each child cut open the top of his or her pumpkin and scoop out the inside. Have children investigate inside their pumpkins and compare the interiors with the exteriors. Ask students to write down their observations and comparisons.

7. After their observations are complete, help children draw or carve faces into their pumpkins to make jack-o'-lanterns to bring home.

Pumpkin Pie Recipe

Materials:
- 1 1/2 cups canned or mashed cooked pumpkin
- 3/4 cup sugar
- 1/2 teaspoon salt
- 1 teaspoon cinnamon
- 1/2 teaspoon ginger
- 1/4 teaspoon nutmeg
- 1/4 teaspoon cloves
- 3 slightly beaten eggs
- 1 1/4 cups milk
- 1 6-ounce can of evaporated milk
- 1 9" unbaked pastry shell
- wooden spoon
- large mixing bowl

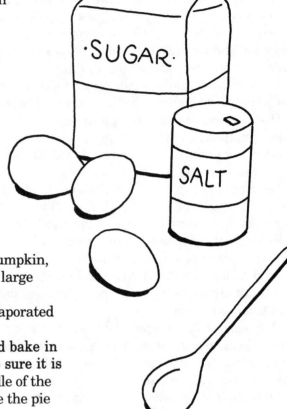

Directions:
1. Ask a small group of children to mix together the pumpkin, sugar, salt, cinnamon, ginger, nutmeg, and cloves in a large mixing bowl.

2. Let another small group add the eggs, milk, and evaporated milk and blend well.

3. Pour the mixture into the unbaked pastry shell and bake in a 400°F oven for approximately 50 minutes. To make sure it is cooked through, test by inserting a knife into the middle of the pie. If any of the mixture comes out on the knife, place the pie back in the oven for several more minutes.

Jack-O'-Lantern Faces

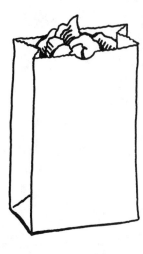

Materials:
- ◆ paper lunch bags
- ◆ newspapers
- ◆ black yarn
- ◆ orange, brown, and black paint
- ◆ decorating materials

Directions:
1. Give each child a paper lunch bag. Have children stuff the bags with newspaper and tie at the top with black yarn, as shown.

2. Tell children to paint the bags orange and the tops of the bags brown.

3. When the paint has dried, give children black paint to paint features on their pumpkins. Children may also wish to use various types of decorating materials (yarn, buttons, glitter, stickers) to personalize their pumpkins.

4. Place the pumpkins on windowsills around the room as Halloween decorations.

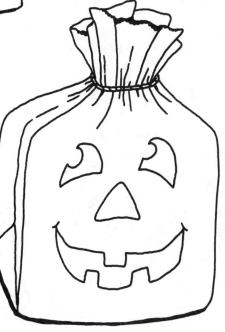

Halloween Class Party Tips

Have a meeting with the class on what type of party they would like to have to celebrate Halloween. Discuss what types of activities they would like to do, which foods they would like to serve, and whom to invite. Write the comments on experience chart paper. Help children make group decisions by taking a vote when the class is undecided on a resolution.

Set up committees to handle planning, production, decorations, activities, and food preparation. Supervise the planning, intervening only when necessary.

Make invitations using the patterns on pages 71-72. Children may invite a parent, or another adult family member or friend.

Some suggested foods to serve:
- ◆ cupcakes frosted to look like jack-o'-lanterns
- ◆ "blood punch" (a cherry or strawberry punch)
- ◆ carrot and raisin salad
- ◆ sugar cookies shaped like Halloween figures and frosted orange

Some suggested classroom decorations:
- ◆ flying ghosts hung from the lights
- ◆ Jack-O'-Lantern faces (see page 69)
- ◆ Halloween place mats (using the figures on pages 71-73)

Some suggested activities:
- ◆ pin the tail on the black cat
- ◆ bobbing for apples
- ◆ a feely box (use spaghetti for worms, mashed gelatin for brains, peeled grapes for eyeballs)
- ◆ recite poems and songs

A Very Scary Bulletin Board

Materials:

- ◆ crayons and markers
- ◆ scissors
- ◆ construction paper
- ◆ dark blue bulletin board paper
- ◆ stapler or tape
- ◆ glow-in-the-dark Halloween stickers

Directions:

1. Reproduce the Halloween figure patterns on pages 71-73 several times. Ask the children to color the figures and cut them out.

2. Ask children to use construction paper to make additional pictures for the board.

3. Cover the bulletin board with dark paper so that it resembles nighttime. Staple or tape the pictures in place. Add glow-in-the-dark stickers if desired.

4. Have each child write a short, scary story about one or more of the figures on the bulletin board.

5. Arrange the stories around the pictures for visitors and other students to read and enjoy.

A Very Scary Story

Sit the class in a circle around a glowing jack-o'-lantern with the lights off. The leader begins a story about Halloween and stops after one or two sentences. The next child in the circle picks up the story and adds a few more sentences. Children should try to create their additions based on what the child before him or her said.

After everyone has had a chance to contribute to the story, have each child draw a picture about his or her own part in it. Children may write or dictate the text for their illustrations on each page. Put the pages together to make a scary class book for the reading center.

Halloween Pop-Up Book

Materials:
- ◆ 12" x 24" construction paper
- ◆ pencil
- ◆ scissors
- ◆ crayons and markers
- ◆ glue

Directions:

1. Give each child a piece of construction paper and demonstrate how to fold it in half widthwise.

2. Have each child mark off two lines, about 2" apart and 3" long, in the middle of the fold. Then help each child cut the lines, as shown.

3. Demonstrate how to open the paper and gently pull the cut section out so that when the paper is folded again, the tab will fold into the paper as shown.

4. Let each child choose one of the Halloween figure patterns on pages 71–73 to use to make a book. Reproduce the selected pattern once for each child.

5. Have students color the figures and cut them out. Then show the children how to glue each figure to the vertical section of the tab so that it appears to be standing out from the background, as shown.

6. Lay the paper flat and draw a background and foreground for the character. When the paper is folded again, gently pull the tab in again.

7. Have each child glue the inside of the book into another piece of paper, folded in half the same way. Children may wish to design covers for their books and give them titles.

Halloween Then and Now

Tell the class that there are many legends about how Halloween began. Some people say that in England, thousands of years ago, there was a holiday called "Summer's End." On this day people would thank the sun for their good harvest by decorating their homes with fruits and vegetables. But some people believed that in the evening before this day, ghosts and witches would come out to cause harm and fear. To keep the ghosts away, people built huge bonfires up on hills. They cut holes in turnips and put candles inside them to scare away these terrible creatures.

Explain that today, people do not really believe in ghosts and witches. Instead they pretend to be scary monsters and dress up in costumes. Children go from house-to-house "trick-or-treating." If the person at home does not give out a treat, then the children may play a trick on that person. Many children today go trick-or-treating for a short while, and then go to Halloween parties where they play games and eat candy and other treats.

Reinforce to the class that it is important to follow a few safety rules when trick-or-treating. Share the following information with the class.

1. Never trick-or-treat alone. Take along a friend, a parent, or a sibling.
2. Never go inside someone's home while trick-or-treating. Wait for your treats outside.
3. Do not eat anything until one of your parents has inspected it.
4. Wear reflective patches on your costume when trick-or-treating in the evening. Also, bring a flashlight.
5. If you cannot trick-or-treat in your area, consider inviting some friends over for a Halloween party in your home.

Halloween Card

Materials:
- ◆ crayons and markers
- ◆ scissors
- ◆ construction paper
- ◆ glue

Directions:

1. Reproduce the Halloween figures on page 78 once for each child. Have students color the figures and cut them out.

2. Ask each child to fold a 9" x 12" piece of paper in half widthwise. Glue the werewolf or ghost to the front of the card as shown.

3. Encourage the children to draw a scene or decorations around their Halloween characters.

4. Have each student write special Halloween messages to the recipient of the card before signing his or her own name.

Best Books About Halloween

◆ *Georgie's Halloween*, written by Robert Bright (Doubleday, 1971)

◆ *Ghost's Hour, Spook's Hour*, written by Eve Bunting (Clarion, 1987)

◆ *Joey the Jack O'-Lantern*, written by Janet Craig (Troll, 1988)

◆ *Henrietta's Halloween*, written by Syd Hoff (Garrard, 1980)

◆ *The Mystery of the Flying Orange Pumpkin*, written by Steven Kellogg (Dial, 1983)

◆ *Teeny Witch and the Great Halloween Ride*, written by Liz Matthews (Troll, 1991)

◆ *Henry and Mudge Under the Yellow Moon*, written by Cynthia Rylant (Macmillan, 1992)

◆ *That Terrible Halloween Night*, written by James Stevenson (Greenwillow, 1980)

◆ *Heckedy Peg*, written by Audrey Wood (Harcourt Brace Jovanovich, 1987)

◆ *Ghost Train*, written by Stephen Wyllie (Dial, 1992)

Name _____

Campaign Fever

Election Day is the first Tuesday in November. On this day we vote for people running for different government offices in our towns, cities, counties, states, and country.

This boy and girl have made up a campaign poster. Use the key below to figure out what their Election Day message is.

We Promise

| 12 | 8 | 14 | 14 | 8 | 15 |

| 6 | 11 | 20 | 17 | 17 | 3 |

| 3 | 24 | 19 | 11 | 20 | 8 | 6 |

8 + 7 = R	11 + 9 = H	15 - 3 = B	10 + 14 = U
15 - 9 = S	6 + 5 = C	12 + 7 = N	19 - 5 = T
16 - 8 = E	9 + 8 = O	10 - 7 = L	

Fall Bookmarks

Celebrate National Children's Book Week (the third week in November) by making these bookmarks with the class.

Materials:
- glue
- oaktag
- crayons or markers
- scissors
- hole puncher
- yarn

Directions:
1. Reproduce the bookmarks on page 82 once for each child.
2. Help each child mount the bookmarks on oaktag, then have the children color and cut them out.
3. Punch a hole at the top of each bookmark.
4. Have children thread short lengths of yarn through the holes.

To celebrate National Children's Book Week during the third week in November, arrange for a class trip to the town library. Request that children bring their own library cards, or ask permission from parents to submit an application for any child who does not have a card.

Go over rules for library behavior before departing. Remind children that libraries are places for people to read and study quietly, and that all books should be treated with care and put back in their proper places.

When you arrive at the library, show children the different sections of the children's room. Give a brief explanation of the Dewey decimal system and how people can use the card catalog to find books about specific subjects or books written by favorite authors. Ask volunteers to name a subject or author and then show children how it may be looked up in the card catalog.

Have a librarian or other library worker tell the class about some of the children's programs that are offered by the library, such as reading clubs, story hours, craft lessons, holiday parties, films, and so on.

If possible, let each child take out one book on his or her card. After the class returns to the school, ask each child to write a few sentences describing what his or her favorite part of the library is and what types of books he or she likes best.

Reading
Brings You To
New Heights

Share A Book
With A
Friend

Name _____

  # Alphabetical Mix-Up

Help the librarian get these 10 books back on the shelves by putting them in alphabetical order according to the author's last name. Write a 1 next to the first book, a 2 next to the second book, and so on.

Silly Sam by Waldo Wackymeister _____

Who's on First? by Hugo Last _____

The Kid Who Only Ate Ice Cream by Z. Z. Cone _____

A Most Beautiful Day by Sonny Sky _____

I Thought I Was a Cat by Ima Feline _____

See the Future by Crystal Ball _____

Mondays Are the Worst by Freddy Friday _____

The Monsters Are Coming! by Frank N. Stein _____

A Million Laughs by Jolly Parton _____

Clown College by B. A. Bozo _____

Plymouth Plantation Play Set

Materials:
◆ crayons and markers
◆ scissors
◆ oaktag
◆ tape
◆ construction paper scraps

Directions:
1. Reproduce the Plymouth Plantation patterns on pages 86-87 several times. Ask children to help color the figures and cut them out.

2. Choose an area where the play set will not be disturbed, such as a table away from the main flow of traffic.

3. Help children tape or staple a 3" oaktag loop to the bottom of the back of each figure to make it stand up, as shown.

4. Tape the fences together to create longer lengths.

5. For added realism, encourage children to create the nearby Atlantic Ocean and woods, and items within the village, such as streets and gardens. Children may also wish to create the *Mayflower* and anchor it out in the ocean.

6. To help children re-create the events of the first Thanksgiving, share the information on page 85 with the students.

The First Thanksgiving

The Pilgrims left England because they wanted to be free to practice their own religion. First they headed to Holland, hoping their religious practice would be allowed, but they soon had to leave there as well.

The Pilgrims sailed from Holland to America in 1620. The ride over in the *Mayflower* was crowded, food and water supplies were low, and disease spread among the people. Many Pilgrims died on the long trip. The passengers had no rooms to themselves. They spent their days and nights on the floor or wherever they could find room. There were no bathrooms, and no privacy at all.

The trip took three long months. When they finally sighted land, the Pilgrims were very happy. They arrived in December. The people had to live on their ship until houses were built on land. More people died during the harsh, cold winter.

The Native Americans who were living nearby wanted to help the Pilgrims. They sent Squanto, a Native American who spoke English, to talk to the Pilgrims. Soon the Native Americans were helping the Pilgrims plant seeds, hunt, and fish. They helped the remaining Pilgrim settlers stay alive. To show their gratitude, the Pilgrims and Native Americans held a three-day feast in late November, serving such foods as fish, popcorn, breads, meats, and vegetables.

Today we celebrate Thanksgiving on the fourth Thursday in November. We remember and honor the Pilgrims, and the Native Americans who helped them survive.

Butter Recipe

Explain to the class that when the Pilgrims first came to America, they had to make their own butter. The Pilgrims had a device called a butter churn in which they would place the cream and pound it until it formed butter.

Make this butter recipe with the class to re-create what it was like for the Pilgrims to obtain their foods without the conveniences of modern-day life.

Materials:

- ◆ pint of heavy cream
- ◆ salt
- ◆ jar with tight lid
- ◆ plastic knives
- ◆ paper plates
- ◆ crackers

Directions:
1. Pour the heavy cream into a jar with a tight lid.
2. Give each child a chance to shake the jar for a minute or two. Tell students to be patient, because the butter takes about five minutes of hard shaking before it forms.
3. The butter is done when a lumpy ball is formed surrounded by a liquid. Skim off the liquid. Tell the children that this liquid is called buttermilk.
4. If desired, sprinkle a pinch of salt onto the butter and mix it in.
5. Place a little bit of the butter onto a plate for each child. Distribute plastic knives and crackers.

Turkey Hand Puppet

Materials:

- ◆ crayons and markers
- ◆ 9" paper plates
- ◆ scissors
- ◆ construction paper
- ◆ glue
- ◆ collage materials
- ◆ stapler

Directions:

1. Distribute a paper plate to each child. Ask the children to color the backs of the paper plates.

2. Using the construction paper, have students design feathers for their turkey puppets. Or, have the children use real feathers. Glue the feathers in place around the uncolored side of the paper plate, as shown.

3. To make the turkey's face, children should cut a head and neck from construction paper, then add features using crayons, markers, or collage materials. Glue the head to the side opposite the one having no feathers, as shown.

4. Tell each student to make feet for the turkey out of construction paper. Then glue the feet in place on the edge that has no feathers.

5. Give each child one more paper plate and demonstrate how to place the two plates together with the fronts facing each other. Then staple the plates together around the edges of both plates, leaving approximately 4" free along the bottom, as shown.

6. Show children how to slip their hands inside the puppets. If desired, have students make up poems or songs to perform using their turkey puppets.

Name _____

Native American Symbols Message

Native Americans used symbols like the ones below to write messages and stories. Use the symbols to write sentences using Native American symbols and English words.

_____

_____

_____

_____

Thanksgiving Class Party Tips

Tell the class that Thanksgiving is a time to think about all the good things we have, and the people with whom we share our lives. Plan a party with the class to reflect this feeling of thankfulness.

Assign children to various committees, such as food, decorations, activities, and invitations. Include as many of the children's families, foods, and activities as possible. Create lists showing all the suggestions made by the committees and choose a few from each for the party.

Before sitting down to eat, ask children and guests alike to name one thing for which they are thankful. It could be something as simple as a toy or as deep as love for their families.

Squirrel Paper-Bag Puppet

Materials:
- crayons and markers
- scissors
- paper lunch bags
- glue
- collage materials

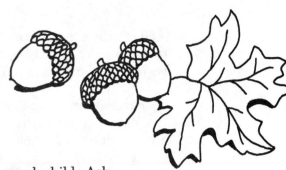

Directions:

1. Reproduce the squirrel patterns once for each child. Ask students to color the patterns and cut them out.

2. Show the children how to glue the squirrel's head to the bottom of a paper lunch bag, facing the crease.

3. Next, have each child glue the body to the short side of the bag, under the squirrel head. Glue the tail to the back of the bag.

4. Children may wish to add details such as yarn for whiskers, buttons for eyes or a nose, and beads for acorns to be held in the squirrel's paws.

5. Teach the class the following poem about squirrels. Let children use their puppets when reciting the poem.

A Squirrel's Busy Day

Running, jumping, here and there,
In the trees, and everywhere.
Finding nuts to hide away,
I'll save them for another day.
Chattering loudly, can't you hear?
With my friends, far and near.
If you see me as you go,
Be sure to stop and say, "Hello!"

GLUE HERE

Nocturnal Animals

Share some books about animals with the class. Have children note that some animals prefer to be awake at night and others prefer to work and play during the day. Identify some night animals and some day animals with the class. Explain that some animals have special characteristics that have helped them adapt to night life. Owls have large eyes to help let in more light for better vision at night, and bats use echoes to find out how close or far away something is. This helps them navigate in the dark.

Divide a large sheet of butcher paper in half with a dark marker. Label one side of the sheet "Night" and the other side, "Day." Ask two volunteers to draw a picture of the moon and stars and a picture of the sun next to the appropriate heading.

Distribute old magazines and workbooks to the class. Ask the children to cut out pictures of each type of animal. When each student has collected a few pictures, let the child glue the animals to the butcher paper under the correct heading.

Migration Time

Ask the class if they have noticed that in the winter there seem to be fewer birds around the neighborhood. Ask why they think birds might leave the area and where the birds might go. Write the children's comments on experience chart paper.

Make a telescope with the class to use on a bird walk to help them see birds close-up. Give each child a cardboard paper-towel roll. Let students decorate the rolls any way they choose, using crayons and markers, construction paper designs, or collage materials glued to the outside.

Take a short walk outside the school looking for different types of birds that frequent the area. After the walk, encourage students to research their finds in reference books about birds, and discover the names of the various birds and any characteristics unique to those birds.

During the winter, take another walk and ask students to look for those same birds. Help the class do more research to find out why some of the birds are no longer around and where they went. Encourage students to think logically by asking them questions such as:

◆ If you were a bird, would you want to stay in cooler or warmer climates? Why?
◆ What kinds of foods do birds eat? Are these foods available during the colder months of the year?
◆ Where do you think the birds went?
◆ When do you think the birds will come back?

Answers

Page 19:
I pledge allegiance to the flag of the United States of America and to the republic for which it stands, one nation under God, indivisible, with liberty and justice for all.

Pages 24 and 25:

6 = Saskatchewan	16 = New Brunswick
8 = Newfoundland	18 = Manitoba
9 = Northwest Territories	20 = Quebec
10 = Ontario	21 = Nova Scotia
13 = Yukon Territory	25 = Alberta
14 = Prince Edward Island	26 = British Columbia

Page 32:
1. yellow 2. blue 3. red 4. green 5. brown
6. orange 7. white 8. black

Page 33:
1. The Jewish New Year is called Rosh Hashanah.
2. People go to temple and say prayers. 3. The trumpet is called a shofar. 4. The trumpet reminds people to gather in the synagogue. 5. They celebrate with special dinners. 6. People eat challah bread, gefilte fish, and apples with honey.

Page 41:
Dial 911. Stop, drop, and roll.

Page 44:
Objects that sink: dough, paper clips, marbles, pennies, rocks. Objects that float: sponges, straws, rubber bands, corks, paper, aluminum foil, pencils.

Page 47:
1492: hourglass, axe, armor, quill, map.
Today: television, cassette player with headphones, computer, rollerblades, watch.

Page 58:
1. 4 yard line 2. 21 yard line 3. 23 yard line
4. 29 yard line 5. 49 yard line 6. 39 yard line
7. 48 yard line 8. 52 yards

Page 59:

Panthers:	0	1	2	0	0	4	0	0	2	Total: 9
Stars:	0	3	0	1	0	0	2	2	2	Total: 10

Page 60:
12:00, 3:30, 8:00, 11:00, 5:30, 9:15

Page 80:
Better school lunches.

Page 83:
10, 6, 3, 8, 4, 1, 5, 9, 7, 2